INSIDE
WEATHER

by Mary Kay Carson

Illustrations by Cynthia Shaw

STERLING CHILDREN'S BOOKS
New York

STERLING CHILDREN'S BOOKS
New York
An Imprint of Sterling Publishing
387 Park Avenue South
New York, NY 10016

© 2011 by Mary Kay Carson

Designed by Anke Stohlmann Design.

ISBN 978-1-4027-5881-2 (hardcover)
ISBN 978-1-4027-8948-9 (flexibound)

Distributed in Canada by Sterling Publishing
c/o Canadian Manda Group, 165 Dufferin Street
Toronto, Ontario, Canada M6K 3H6
Distributed in the United Kingdom by GMC Distribution Services
Castle Place, 166 High Street, Lewes, East Sussex, England BN7 1XU
Distributed in Australia by Capricorn Link (Australia) Pty. Ltd.
P.O. Box 704, Windsor, NSW 2756, Australia

For information about custom editions, special sales, and premium and corporate purchases, please contact Sterling Special Sales at 800-805-5489 or specialsales@sterlingpublishing.com.

Printed in China
Lot#:
10 9 8 7 6 5 4 3 2
03/14

www.sterlingpublishing.com/kids

IMAGE CREDITS:

Alamy: © Prisma Bildagentur AG: 4-9; © Ernest Rice: 26; © A ROOM WITH VIEWS: 36 top; © Ryan McGinnis: 42 left; © Dennis MacDonald: 42 right

Corbis: © Mike Hollingshead/Science Faction: front cover; © Wayne Lynch/All Canada Photos: 1; © Kenji Kondo/epa: 15 right; © Seth Resnick/Science Faction: 16; © RICK WILKING/Reuters: 19-20; © Jim Reed: 27-28 left; © Ashley Cooper: 28 bottom right; © Jim Reed: 31; © Mike Hollingshead/Science Faction: 33; © Theo Allofs: 34 top; © JS Productions: 34 bottom; © Jim Reed/Science Faction: 39 middle; © Jim Reed: 45 top

Getty: © Per Breiehagen: 35 top; © Ed Darack: 35 bottom; © Gary Williams/Liaison: 37 right

iStockphoto: © Chanyut Sribuarawd: back cover; © Tamara Volodina: 2-3; © Dmitry Rogozhin: 5; © Eric Foltz: 6 top; © Roberto A Sanchez: 6 bottom; © Jens Klingebiel: 7 top; © Earl Eliason: 7 bottom; © Nataliia Maiboroda: 8; © Sergey Borisov: 10-11; © Jan Rihak: 15 left; © Olga Galkina: 22; © morkeman: 27 top left; © Jan Ellen Ball: 27 top right; © Don Komarechka: 27 middle left; © Gianluca Padovani: 28 middle left; © Vitali Dyatchenko: 28 middle right; © Jowita Stachowiak: 28 bottom left; © Ljupco Smokovski: 32 right; © Josef Becker: 43 top; © Ron and Patty Thomas Photography: 43-44; © Floriano Rescigno: 44 bottom

NASA: SOHO/MDI, SOHO/EIT, and SOHO/LASCO (ESA & NASA): 11 right; Marit Jentoft-Nilsen, based on data from NOAA GOES: 12; Earth Observatory imagery created by Jesse Allen: 30 bottom

National Oceanic and Atmospheric Administration (NOAA): 30 top; NOAA/GTMNERR: 38; NOAA/ESRL: 39 left; 40

Photo Researchers, Inc: © Rafael Macia: 27 middle right; © Howard Bluestein: 27-28 right; © Kent Wood: 32 left; © James Steinberg: 36 bottom; © Roger Hill: 37 left; © "David Parker / European Space Agency: 39 right

University Corporation for Atmospheric Research (UCAR): 45 bottom

HOW'S YOUR WEATHER?

Weather affects everyone. How did you decide what to wear today? The temperature likely played a part. Will your team practice outside or inside today? Rain might make that decision for you. Weather affects people in more serious ways, too. Severe weather like floods, lightning, extreme heat and cold, hurricanes, and tornadoes kill thousands of people every year. Rainfall makes or breaks crop harvests, snowstorms can collapse roofs, and floods can wash out bridges. In some ways, weather doesn't impact our everyday lives as much as it once did. Modern heat and air-conditioning control temperatures. Cars and buses shelter us from downpours while we move from place to place. Today's technology constantly tracks weather conditions, giving us time to prepare for dangerous storms or a deep freeze. However, because our world is now connected by highways and airline flight paths, the effects of severe weather can be felt by people thousands of miles away. A blizzard in London can stop airline flights worldwide. A tornado-damaged factory in China can create a shortage of computer chips in the United States.

Weather tracking and predictions are more important than ever in today's connected world. Yet while the information gathering and study of weather grows more sophisticated, long-term forecasts are becoming harder to make. Why? Global climate change is altering the ingredients that go into the weather mix.

Cars, trees, and power lines became part of a giant ice sculpture along Lake Geneva in Switzerland when strong winds splashed water over its shoreline.

CLIMATE VS. WEATHER

What is weather, exactly? It's what's going on outside in a particular place at a specific time. The moisture, heat, and pressure of the air mix and blend, churn and separate to create weather. These ingredients cook up a windy day, stormy night, or sunny morning.

One thing weather is not, is climate. The two words are often used as if they mean the same thing, but they are actually different. *Weather* describes a particular place at a specific time—what it's like outside now. *Climate* describes a place's pattern of weather over a long period—what it's usually like outside. Death Valley in California has a hot desert climate, for example. But today's weather there might be cool and rainy. Weather changes from one day to the next, but climate does not.

Death Valley National Park has a desert climate.

World Climate Zones

What makes a desert hot and dry while a rainforest is hot and wet? The kind of climate a particular place has depends on many factors. How far it is from the equator (its latitude) is important. Sweaty tropical climates wrap Earth's equator like a belt. Chilly tundra and arctic climates are found around the North and South poles. Another factor is altitude, or how high a place is. Even Hawaii has snow on its highest mountaintops.

Warm Summer Continental

Dry summers and wind-whipped wildfires keep prairies and other grasslands free of trees. The roots of prairie grasses often grow deeper than the plant is tall. Their deep underground root systems can survive fire and drought. Grazing buffalo, elk, and pronghorn share the prairies with burrowing hares, badgers, and prairie dogs.

Wet Tropical

Year-round rain and heat is the secret to creating a tropical rainforest overflowing with layers of life. It has the greatest diversity of species of any place on Earth, from monkeys and colorful parrots to towering trees and enormous ant colonies.

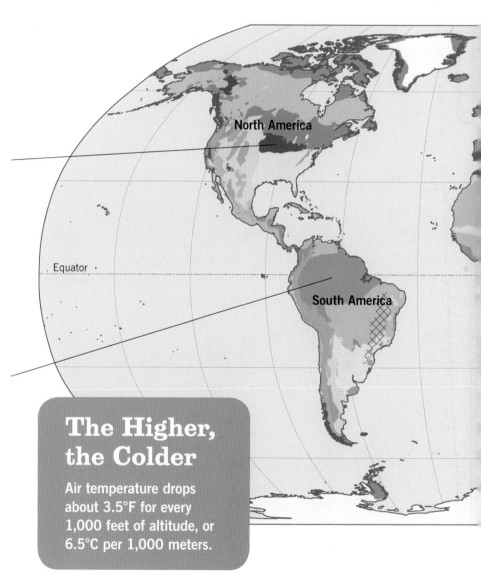

The Higher, the Colder

Air temperature drops about 3.5°F for every 1,000 feet of altitude, or 6.5°C per 1,000 meters.

This map shows Earth's patchwork of climate zones. A region's temperature, moisture, and vegetation classify it. There are six general climate types, each of which includes more specific kinds of climates.

CONTENTS

How to read this book

This book is different from most books you read. Many of its pages fold out—or flip up! To know where to read next, follow arrows like these ⬆, and look for page numbers to help you find your place. Happy exploring!

How close to an ocean or a large lake a place is influences climate, too. Water cools and warms slowly, keeping the temperatures of seas steadier than land and making coastal regions milder. A final factor is where a region lies within the global patterns of wind that circulate the air. Regular winds blow dry air to the North African desert—the Sahara, for example.

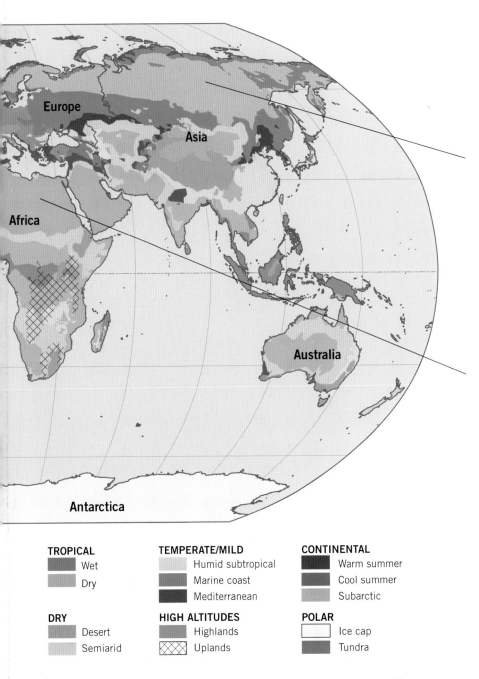

Europe

Asia

Africa

Australia

Antarctica

TROPICAL
Wet
Dry

DRY
Desert
Semiarid

TEMPERATE/MILD
Humid subtropical
Marine coast
Mediterranean

HIGH ALTITUDES
Highlands
Uplands

CONTINENTAL
Warm summer
Cool summer
Subarctic

POLAR
Ice cap
Tundra

Subarctic

Long, cold winters and short, rainy summers define this enormous climate zone. Its evergreen forests of mostly fir and spruce trees stretch across Canada, Alaska, northern Europe, and Russia. Minks, wolverines, lynx, and wolves live in these dense forests.

Desert

Almost no rain and hot temperatures create North Africa's Sahara. Few plants cover its driest sand dunes and gravel plains. Areas a bit less harsh are home to desert-adapted gerbils, lizards, antelope, and camels.

WHY AND HOW DOES WEATHER HAPPEN?

Why are some days sweaty hot while others are icicle cold? When does rain change to snow? What makes a storm kick out lightning? How does a cloud make hail? The short answer is *sun*, *air*, and *water*. These three ingredients are behind all of our world's weather.

Coldest Ever

The coldest recorded temperature on Earth was -128.6°F (-89.2°C) on July 21, 1983, at Vostok station, Antarctica.

Hottest Ever

The hottest recorded temperature on Earth was 136°F (57.8°C) on September 13, 1922, in El Azizia, Libya.

It takes about eight minutes for the sun's light to reach Earth.

Frequent Flyers

Bad weather contributes to about 30 percent of all air-travel accidents.

EARTH'S CHANGING CLIMATE: WHAT IS GLOBAL CLIMATE CHANGE?

While weather is always changing, climate stays the same. At least, it's supposed to. Earth's climate is now changing—it's warming. That's why global climate change (GCC) is also often called global warming.

Earth's climate has changed throughout its four-billion-year history. The dinosaurs lived on a hotter planet than we do, and then there was a chilly ice age 10,000 years ago. But these were slow, gradual changes over many millennia. The current rapid rise in Earth's temperature is only during the past 100 years or so. The increase mirrors the rise of human-created pollution from burning coal, oil, and gas. Using fossil fuels like these adds carbon dioxide to the air. Carbon dioxide is called a greenhouse gas, because like a greenhouse, the gas traps the sun's energy and heats things up. Scientists predict that as temperatures continue to rise, ice caps will melt. This will raise the level of the sea and bring more extreme weather, such as droughts, floods, and storms. Earth's climate zones will also shift because of GCC, possibly making cool places warm and wet places dry.

Small Number, Big Deal

The average temperature of Earth is only 1.2 to 1.4°F (0.7 to 0.8°C) warmer than it was a century ago. But that's enough to have caused higher sea levels from more melted polar ice.

All-Powerful Sun

All weather starts with the sun's energy. The sun continually sends light and heat through space toward Earth. About a third of this solar radiation is reflected off Earth and bounced back into space. The air, ocean, and land soak up the other two-thirds and are warmed.

Right now, somewhere it's freezing cold, and somewhere it's burning hot. The sun doesn't evenly warm our planet. Earth's equator receives the strongest, most direct rays from the sun. The poles receive the weakest, least direct sunlight. Think about shining a flashlight at a globe. When shining it at the equator, a perfect circle of bright light appears. When holding the flashlight at the equator but tilting it upward, the light reaches the North Pole. However, the light is now stretched into an oval and is not as bright at its farthest tip—the North Pole. The sun heats Earth in the same way: warmer at the equator and cooler at the poles. Our planet's tilt causes the parts of Earth that receive more direct sunlight to shift as we travel around the sun. That's why summer is hotter than winter.

Tilt and latitude aren't the only reasons Earth is so unevenly heated by the sun: Oceans and other bodies of water warm up (and cool down) more slowly than forests or fields. Snow, ice, and thick clouds reflect much more sunlight back into space than rocks, pastures, or thin clouds. The warmed parts of Earth's surface heat the air above them. Warm air rises. Earth's cooler parts create sinking air. All this sun-driven temperature unevenness moves and mixes another weather ingredient—air.

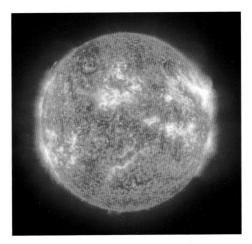

The spacecraft *SOHO* took this blazing hot picture as it flew around the sun.

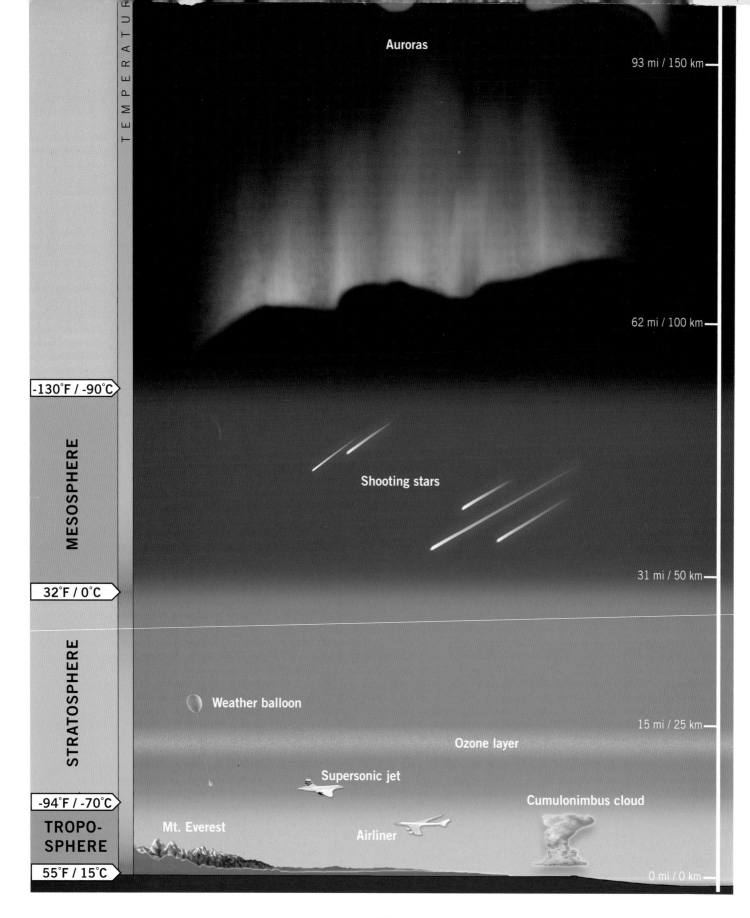

Auroras

93 mi / 150 km

62 mi / 100 km

TEMPERATURE

-130°F / -90°C

MESOSPHERE

Shooting stars

32°F / 0°C

31 mi / 50 km

STRATOSPHERE

Weather balloon

15 mi / 25 km

Ozone layer

Supersonic jet

-94°F / -70°C

Cumulonimbus cloud

TROPO-
SPHERE

Mt. Everest

Airliner

55°F / 15°C

0 mi / 0 km

The Air above Us

Air is odd stuff. It's everywhere but is invisible. Air seems like "nothing," but it is actually a mix of gases that have weight and take up space. (Think of the air filling a balloon as you blow it up.) The gases in air make life on Earth possible. Animals, including you, need oxygen to breathe. Green plants need carbon dioxide to make food for themselves—and to create oxygen. The blanket of air surrounding our planet is called the atmosphere. It reaches from the land and ocean up into space. The part of the atmosphere closest to the surface is the troposphere. (Flip up the page to see it.) This is where weather happens.

The troposphere is full of air that's always changing. Some air is getting hotter and rising, while other air is cooling and sinking. One of the gases in air is water vapor. Air gains and loses water vapor as it heats and cools or moves over oceans and mountains. All this changing and churning in the atmosphere creates wind, clouds, storms, and rain.

Fitting Name

The word *troposphere* means "sphere of change." The prefix *tropo* comes from the Greek word for "turning or change."

What's in Air?

Dry air is mostly nitrogen and oxygen. These two gases make up nearly 99 percent of air, but don't really affect the weather. Argon, carbon dioxide, ozone, and other gases make up just 1 percent. The amount of water vapor in air depends on how moist it is—its humidity. Water vapor is the main weather-making part of air.

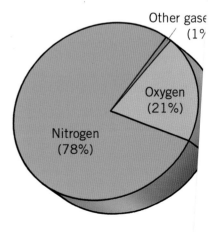

Other gases (1%)

Oxygen (21%)

Nitrogen (78%)

The Atmosphere From Sea to Space

Between down here and outer space is the atmosphere. Scientists divide our atmosphere into four main layers. The lowest is the *troposphere*, where breathable air and weather are located. The *stratosphere* is home to the ozone layer, which protects us from dangerous ultraviolet solar rays. The chilly *mesosphere* is where meteorites are destroyed. In the highest layer, the *thermosphere*, auroras like the northern lights can be found. This layer also contains the ionosphere, a region of charged particles that bounce radio signals around the globe.

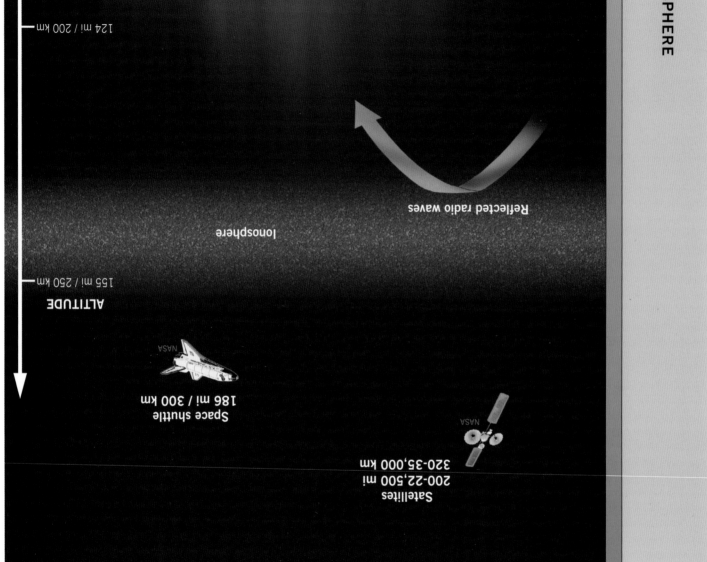

THERMOSPHERE

124 mi / 200 km

Reflected radio waves

Ionosphere

155 mi / 250 km

ALTITUDE

NASA

186 mi / 300 km
Space shuttle

NASA

320-35,000 km
200-22,500 mi
Satellites

The Weight of the Sky

A balloon full of air doesn't weigh much. But the air in the atmosphere all the way up to space does. The atmosphere's weight pushes down on Earth's land and water like blankets stacked on a bed. This pushing down force is called atmospheric pressure, or air pressure. Atmospheric pressure lessens with altitude, or height. There's less air above a mountaintop than below it in a valley.

Air pressure also changes with temperature. A cup of warm air weighs less than a cup of cool air. Why? Heated air molecules move fast, bounce off each other, and spread out, leaving fewer in the cup. The cup of cooled air has slowed down air molecules that are denser, or more tightly packed, so it weighs more.

The weight or pressure of air is important to making weather. Being lighter is why warm air naturally rises—and has a lower pressure. Rising low-pressure air creates clouds and can cause storms. Sinking, heavy, high-pressure air often brings clear skies. Differences in air pressure cause winds, too. Dense, heavy, higher-pressure air pushes toward thinner, lighter lower-pressure air. Whoosh!

Ouch!

Earth's atmosphere constantly pushes down on us with a force of 14.7 pounds (6.7 kg) for every square inch (6.5 square cm) of surface. A lifetime on this planet has made us used to it, so we don't notice it.

The air pressure at sea level is three times as high as on top of Mount Everest. Up there the air is nearly too thin to breathe.

Weighty Number

The weight of Earth's entire atmosphere is about 12,000,000,000,000,000,000 pounds (5,300,000,000,000,000,000 kg). That's the weight of 1,200,000 billion elephants or 40,000 billion blue whales.

Warm Front

A warm front is the boundary between an advancing warm air mass and the cold air mass that it is overtaking. As the lighter warm air crashes into the cold air, it slides up and over the heavier cold air. The rising warm air forms thick clouds that create rain, snow, or sleet.

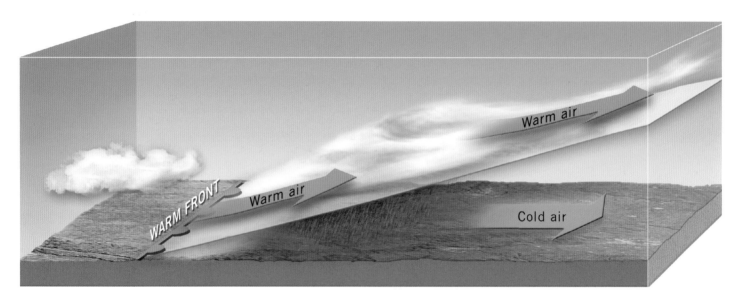

Stationary Front

Sometimes battling air masses reach a standoff—neither advances. This is called a stationary front. Clashing air masses can push and bump against each other with no progress for days in a stationary front. If the air is humid enough, clouds and rain can form as some of the warm air slides over the cold air along the front line. This can bring gloomy, gray, cloudy skies with drizzle or flurries for a week or longer.

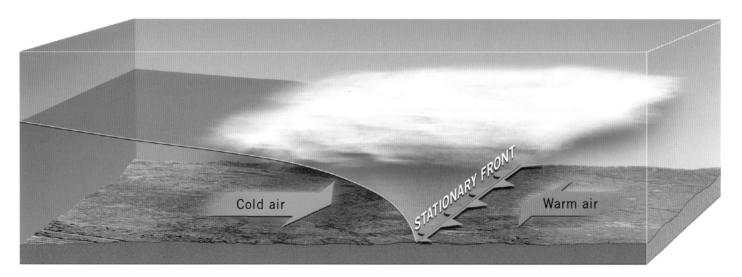

Fronts: Clash of the Air Masses

When two different kinds of air masses meet, they don't mix. They fight it out, like soldiers on the battlefront. The boundary line between the two air masses is called a front—a battleground of weather. Fronts are named for the advancing invader, so a cold front is a cold air mass taking over a warm one. Fronts are weather changers. A cold front passing over your region can turn a hot, hazy heat wave into clear, sunny, dry weather. The battle for change can be rough, though, especially when the crashing air masses have very different temperatures, speeds, or moisture amounts. These strong fronts can bring heavy rain, snow, wind, and storms.

Cold Front

A cold front is the advancing edge of a cold air mass moving into a warm air mass. Cold air weighs more than warm air, so it sinks and shoves under the lighter warm air, pushing it up. The rising warm air cools, creating clouds and maybe rain or snow.

Weather-Making Masses

Hot air above the tropics and cold air above the poles are constantly on the move, trying to balance Earth's uneven temperature. These huge blobs of air are called air masses. An air mass is a giant body of air that has the same temperature and amount of moisture throughout it. The four basic types of air masses are: cold and dry, cold and humid, warm and dry, and warm and humid. A forming air mass adopts its temperature and humidity combination from the surface under it. Air masses created over the oceans are usually humid, while dry air masses are born over land. Likewise, air masses formed over the poles are cold, and those created in the tropics are warm.

An air mass can cover thousands of square miles. It can overlay an entire continent or sea. These massive blobs of air shove, push, and crash into each other as they move around the planet. Where two air masses meet is called a front. Fronts change the weather by creating clouds, rain, storms, and winds. (Open these pages to see fronts in action.)

Fronts can bring severe weather, like this sunset thunderstorm over Miami, Florida.

Air Masses across the Globe

Air masses take on the temperature and humidity of where they form. That's why weather scientists use place names to categorize and classify them using a two-part code.

The first lowercase letter of an air mass code indicates the humidity of the air mass. A *maritime* air mass forms over the humid ocean, while a *continental* air mass forms over dry land. The temperature of an air mass also comes from a place and is represented by the second capital letter(s) of the code. *A*nt*A*rctic and *A*rctic air masses are cold, *P*olar are cool, *T*ropical are warm, and *E*quatorial are very warm.

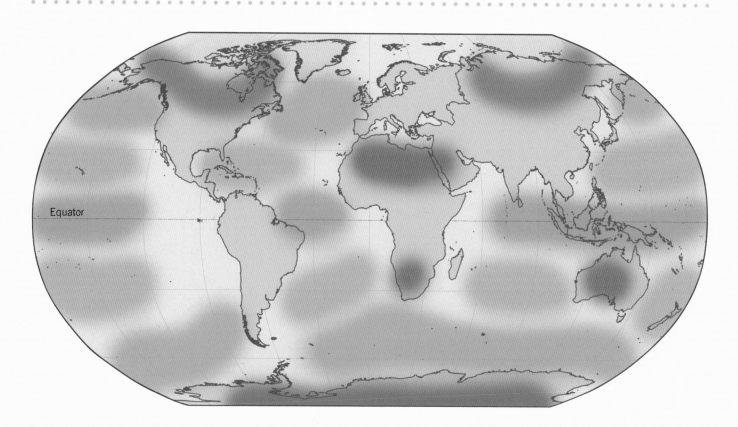

Equator

■ Continental Antarctic (cAA) - very cold & dry
■ Continental Arctic (cA) - cold & dry
■ Continental Polar (cP) - cool & dry
■ Continental Tropical (cT) - warm & dry
■ Maritime Tropical (mT) - warm & moist
■ Maritime Equatorial (mE) - very warm & moist
■ Maritime Polar (mP) - cool & moist

Massive Heat Wave

The Gulf of Mexico is the source of most of the maritime tropical (mT) air in North America, and brings those sweltering summer heat waves east of the Rocky Mountains.

Wind's Way

Winds are named for the direction from which they blow. A north wind comes from the north, for example.

EARTH'S CHANGING CLIMATE: ARE JET STREAMS SHIFTING?

Jet streams are global weather-making winds. These strong winds rush around Earth from west to east in both the Northern and Southern Hemispheres. Jet streams are very high in the atmosphere and often flow between air masses, steering them from above. The position of jet streams affects weather today and in the coming week. A jet stream can lock a warm or cold air mass into place. In the United States, the jet stream often divides colder northern weather from warmer weather south of it.

Jet streams shift from season to season. They flow closer to the poles in summers and closer to the equator in winters. That's normal. But scientists have found that over the past few decades jet streams have moved farther toward the poles overall. "The jet streams mark the edge of the tropics," said atmospheric scientist John Wallace. "So if they are moving poleward that means the tropics are getting wider." That hot belt around the equator will grow bigger. As the hot regions near the equator expand and heat reaches farther distances, it can turn arid land into desert. This could cause deserts like the Sahara to expand. The jet streams' move toward the poles is caused by a warming atmosphere, likely due to climate change.

Why the Winds Blow

Wind is air in motion. Air may be invisible, but you can see what it's doing on a windy day. The molecules of oxygen, nitrogen, and other gases that make up air are not evenly distributed. The air molecules in some places are spread out. In other places, the air molecules are more densely packed. These differences are what make wind because denser air rushes toward less dense, spread-out air. Think of a full bike tire. It's been pumped full of densely packed air. When you open the tire valve, the crowded air blows out to where the air molecules are more spread out.

What causes some air to have more densely packed molecules than other air? Sometimes, like with the tire pump, it's about pressure. For example, the air at sea level is denser than the air on a mountain top because the atmospheric pressure is higher at sea level. The sun's uneven heating of Earth's atmosphere creates areas of air with different densities, too, because cold air is denser than hot air.

Air pressure and temperature both cause differences in air density, so both of these factors can cause wind. High-pressure air flows toward low-pressure air and cool airs flows toward warm air. This continual moving of air circulates our planet's atmosphere and helps determine a place's climate. Local differences in air temperatures create winds that blow from high-pressure areas to lower ones, driving day-to-day weather.

Hurricane Wilma brought serious wind to Naples, Florida, in 2005.

Water World

Earth is a watery blue planet. Oceans alone cover more than 70 percent of its surface. There's also water in our rivers, lakes, streams, ponds, glaciers, sea ice, and in the air. Water vapor is one of the gases in the atmosphere. The air above the United States alone holds some 40 trillion gallons (151 trillion liters) of water.

You probably don't think water is anything special. But it's very unusual stuff. Water is the only substance that naturally occurs on Earth in all three states—solid, liquid, and gas. A cube of gold sitting in a glass on a table doesn't melt into a liquid. But ice does. A pool of ammonia doesn't dry up in the sun and turn into a gas. A puddle of water does. Water changes back and forth into all three states without the heat of blow torches or high-tech deep freezes. This ability to switch easily from ice to liquid to gas creates the water cycle that powers our planet's weather.

Water Go Round

Water is always moving between Earth's atmosphere and its surface. This cycling of water dries up creeks, dumps snow, and soaks plants. The sun drives the water cycle with its heat. Heating changes liquid water in oceans, lakes, rivers, soil, and plant leaves into water vapor through a process called evaporation. Rising water vapor in the air cools, and the water changes back into liquid droplets in clouds through condensation. Growing water droplets in growing clouds fall to the ground as precipitation, like rain, sleet, or snow. Then the cycle begins again, as the sun heats solid and liquid water until it evaporates.

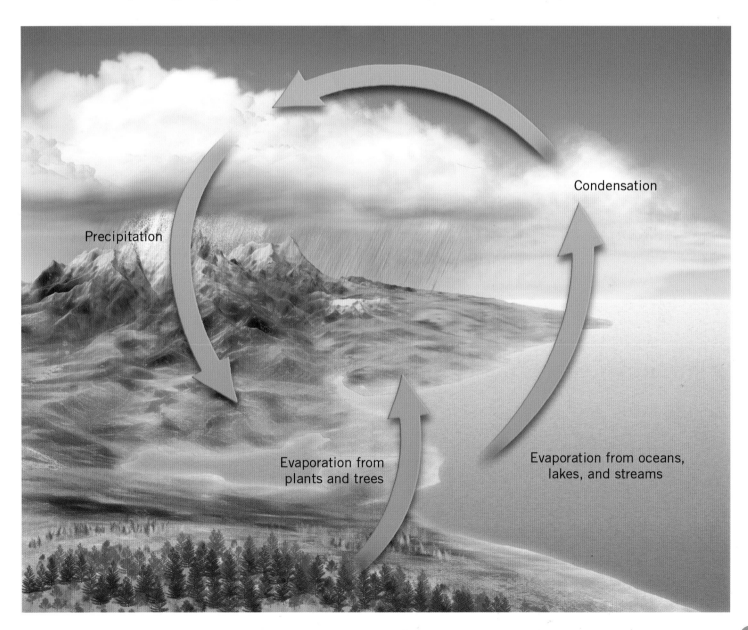

Condensation

Precipitation

Evaporation from plants and trees

Evaporation from oceans, lakes, and streams

Column of Clouds

Clouds are floating clusters of tiny water droplets or ice crystals. Clouds form from rising, cooling, condensing water vapor. They move with the wind and change shape and color with changing conditions, such as temperature, air pressure, and the landscape below. Clouds are affected by weather, create weather, and can give us an idea of what weather is on the way. Identifying clouds is an important part of weather forecasting.

Cloud names are full of information. The basic names of clouds tell you a cloud's shape. Cirrus are wispy and feathery, stratus are layered and flat, and cumulus are lumpy and fluffy. Longer cloud names begin with a prefix that often describes altitude. *Cirro-* is high, while *alto-* is mid-level. Adding *nimbo* to the beginning or end of a cloud name tells you it's making precipitation.

High wispy **cirrus** ice clouds are often seen in clear skies and may mean fair weather will change to rain.

Cirrocumulus clouds are common in winter along with fair, cold weather. But in the tropics, they can mean a hurricane is coming.

Thin-layered high **cirrostratus** are clouds of ice that can mean overcast skies or rain is in the future.

A warm, humid morning sky full of **altostratus** clouds warns of afternoon thunderstorms.

Who's All Wet?

Any form of water that falls out of clouds is precipitation—rain, sleet, hail, snow, drizzle, and so on. When scientists compare amounts of precipitation from place to place or year to year, they include all the different kinds together. The frozen kinds are measured as liquid water. It can take from five to fifteen inches of melted snow to make an inch of rain. Light, fluffy snow has less water than wet, heavy snow.

The kind of precipitation that hits the ground depends on the temperature of the cloud it came from, the temperature of the air it fell through, and the droplets' size. Lift up the page on the right to find out how each kind is made.

American Rain

The continental United States gets enough precipitation yearly to cover the land in 30 inches (0.76 meters) of water.

Thick gray blanket-like **altocumulus** clouds made of ice and water at middle heights are a tip off to rain, snow, or at least, overcast skies.

Giant thunderhead **cumulonimbus** clouds tower to high heights and warn that thunderstorms with heavy rain, hail, winds, and lightning are on the way.

Fluffy lower **cumulus** clouds often "grow" during sunny days and usually mean fair weather unless they grow tall late in the day.

Rebel Cloud

Stratocumulus is a cloud that breaks the rules. Two shapes make up its name.

A sky of **stratocumulus** clouds means dry weather as long as the temperature doesn't drop a lot at night. If it does, then light drizzle or flurries are possible.

Nimbostratus clouds bring rain and snow that can be long lasting.

Flat layers of low **stratus** clouds mean light rain, drizzle, or flurries are likely.

Yearly Precipitation around the Globe

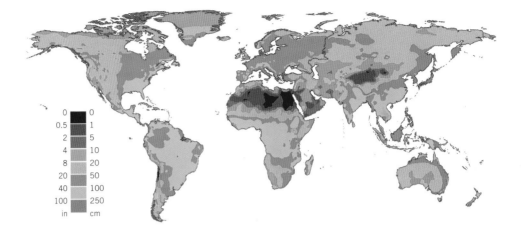

Yearly Precipitation in the United States

Yearly Snowfall in the United States

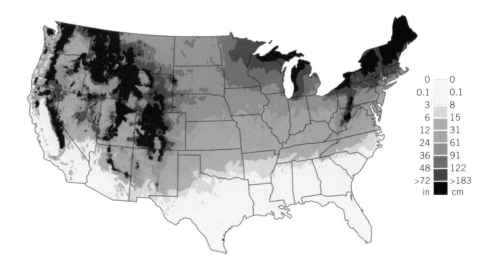

Is it drizzling or raining? Is that white stuff snow or frost? What's the difference between sleet and freezing rain? Find out!

Falling drops of water bigger than 0.02 inches in diameter (.5 mm) are called **rain**, while smaller drops are called **drizzle**.

Freezing rain is rain or drizzle that instantly turns into ice when it hits the ground or any other object.

Snow is made up of crystals of ice in six-sided shapes that often clump into snowflakes.

Drops of rain that freeze into ice pellets in mid-air as they fall through the sky are **sleet**.

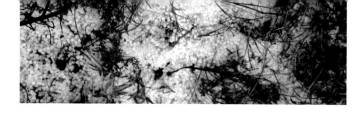

Hail is created inside thunderstorms when added layers of cloud droplets freeze onto balls of ice as strong upward winds repeatedly return them up into the cloud.

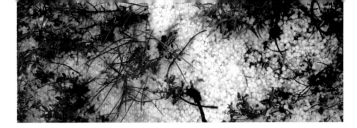

Graupel are white lumpy pellets of ice formed when cloud droplets freeze onto snowflakes.

Fog is a cloud (stratus) on or close to the ground that makes it hard to see.

Dew is water vapor in the air that forms water droplets on grass and other surfaces.

Frost is water vapor in the air that freezes into small ice crystals on surfaces like leaves or windshields.

When frozen water vapor grows into large white ice crystals it's called **hoarfrost**.

WILD WEATHER

You know a storm when you see one. Whipping winds, blinding lightning, heart-stopping thunder, piling snow, and flooding rains. What is a storm, exactly? It's a violent disturbance in the atmosphere that creates hazardous weather. Most storms start from an area of low air pressure surrounded by winds circling inward—a cyclone.

Warm and moist parts of the world have *tropical cyclones*. Tropical cyclones don't have fronts. Instead, their destructive power comes from evaporating warm water and rising heat that fuels a low-pressure monster. Tropical cyclones always begin over the ocean surface in the tropics. These storms form from the bottom up as the warm seawater evaporates, sending heat up into the storm's warm center. Once formed, these storms can move out of the tropics and onto land. The strongest winds are closest to the water or land below. Once a storm's winds reach 74 mph (119 kph), it's called a hurricane, typhoon, or cyclone, depending on where in the world the storm is happening. They are the planet's largest, longest-lasting, and most-destructive storms.

*Extratropical cyclone*s are rotating areas of low pressure that always form outside the tropics. They are storms made from the top down, forming high in the cold upper atmosphere, often along the jet streams. Their high altitude centers are the coldest part of the storm, and their strongest winds happen

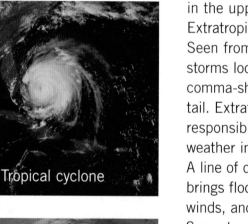
Tropical cyclone

Extratropical cyclone

in the upper atmosphere, too. Extratropical cyclones have fronts. Seen from space, one of these storms looks like a giant white comma-shaped cloud with a long tail. Extratropical cyclones are responsible for much of the bad weather in the middle latitudes. A line of clouds along the tail often brings flooding rain, hail, strong winds, and creates tornadoes. Snowstorms and ice storms can also develop in the center of an extratropical cyclone.

Storms frustrate travelers, destroy billions of dollars in property, and kill thousands of people a year. So what good are they? They help to even out the temperature of Earth's atmosphere. The tropics get more sunlight and heat than the poles. Air near Earth's surface heats up more than air halfway to space. Storms move this heat around and mix it up. Hurricanes and other tropical storms yank heat (and moisture) out of the tropics and push it toward the poles. Giant towering thunderstorms pull heat out of the lower atmosphere and funnel it up into the upper atmosphere.

EARTH'S CHANGING CLIMATE: STORMY FUTURE?

Warmer temperatures are changing our planet's climate. But how will they affect our weather? Scientists believe that global climate change will cause more extreme weather. Why? Heat and moisture power storms, so a warmer world has more storm fuel. Think about tropical cyclones, like hurricanes. Warm seawater creates hurricanes, so warmer oceans that stay warm longer will likely mean more hurricanes. Or, at least, better-fueled, stronger hurricanes.

What about winter storms? Will they show up less as the world warms? Not necessarily in the short term. Why? Cold air can't hold as much moisture as warm air. Not as many water molecules can fit in between the densely packed air molecules in cold air. Some places have temperatures too cold to make much snow, like Antarctica. It's technically a desert. (See the global precipitation map on page 26.) Slightly warmer winter temperatures means air loaded with extra snow-dumping moisture.

Storms are a way Earth balances out its temperature by moving heat toward colder areas. So with more heat to move around, more stormy weather is likely in our future.

Alien Storms

Earth isn't the only stormy place. Mars has dust storms; Jupiter has a storm centuries old; and the sun has really hot solar storms that erupt with flares of magnetic energy.

Giant thunderstorms like this one over the Kansas prairie throw out bolts of lightning, as well as strong winds, drenching rain, and hail.

Glory

A glory is a glorious pale ring of multi-colored light on top of clouds. It is caused when sunlight hits water droplets in the clouds, loops around inside the round drops, and then comes back toward you, splitting the sun's white light into colors along the way. Glories can be hard to see because you need to look down on clouds that have a shadow cast on them. Standing atop a sunny mountain looking down on your own shadow cast on fog below is one way to see glories. It is also possible to see them from airplanes. You need to sit on the shady side of the airplane so the plane casts a shadow on the clouds below your window.

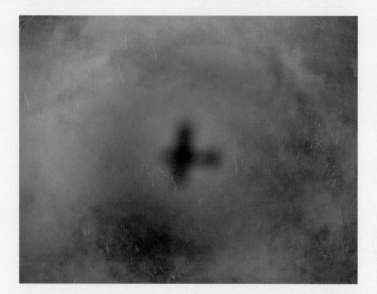

Sun Dog

These solar pets are often seen guarding the sun on one or both sides when the sun is low in the sky. They show up when sunlight hits large six-sided ice crystals in cirrus clouds. The crystals bend the light, bouncing it to the left and right of the sun. Sun dogs are also called mock suns or parhelia (par-HEEL-yuh).

Weird Weather Phenomena

Weather isn't just scary storms and complicated forecasts. Some weather events are beautiful, like rainbows, or eerie, like ball lightning. What causes these spectacular shows in the sky?

Ball Lightning

Ball lightning is an electrically charged ball of air that comes down out of a thunderstorm cloud. It can explode in the air or when it hits something, or it can just fizzle out. This usually red, yellow, or orange phenomenon is less than a foot (30 cm) across and can roll down hills and float down chimneys! It can make a hissing noise and leave behind a foul rotten-egg smell. Ball lightning is very rare, and how it forms is still a mystery.

Rainbow

Nothing's nicer than seeing a rainbow at the end of a storm. If you live in the tropics, though, a rainbow can mean a storm's on the way. That's because to see a rainbow you must be standing with the sun behind you while facing rainfall in another part of the sky. In the middle latitudes, such as in the United States, storms usually come from the west. So after an afternoon storm, while the sun is beginning its descent in the west, you're likely to see a rainbow if you're looking east with the storm moving away from you. In the tropics where storms usually come from the east, standing with the sun at your back in the west means you'll be looking at the rain on its way. What makes a rainbow? Raindrops act like tiny prisms, splitting sunlight into all its colors. A rainbow appears to have an arch shape because you only see half of the full circle. The rest of the circle is hidden below the horizon.

Storms of All Sorts

The world is a stormy place. Have you found yourself in the middle of any of these types of storms? Watch out!

Thunder Storms

Earth experiences as many as 50,000 thunderstorms a day. These common storms bring drenching rain, hail, lightning, thunder, and sometimes tornadoes. Thunderstorms happen when air near the ground is warm, but upper air is cold. As the warm, moist air rises, it cools and begins forming a cloud. If warm, moist, rising air keeps adding to the cloud, a giant cumulonimbus thunderhead develops. Lightning happens when electricity travels between negatively and positively charged parts of a cloud, or between a cloud and the ground. Lightning is how an electrically charged cloud gets rid of its charge. How does a cloud get electrically charged in the first place? Scientists think it happens as upward- and downward-moving water and ice within the thunderhead crash into one another.

Winter Storms

Winter storms bring all kinds of bad weather—snow, sleet, freezing rain, strong winds, and dropping temperatures. Winter storms are tough to forecast. Why? A change of just a few degrees one way or the other can turn rain to sleet or snow to freezing rain. That difference can create a cold rainstorm or a deep snowfall. A winter storm becomes a blizzard if snow is falling, winds are faster than 35 mph (56 km/h), and visibility—how far you can see in front of you—is one-quarter mile (0.4 km) or less.

I Was There! An Elephant Tusk from the Sky

At dusk on April 26, 1989, a tornado tore across the Manikganj District of Bangladesh. The tornado cut a path of destruction up to a mile wide as it moved between—and destroyed—the cities of Daulatpur and Salturia. The twister knocked down buildings, flipped fishing boats, and pulled up trees. It blew mud-and-straw houses into the air with whole families still inside. Every single house within one 2.5 square mile

Icebow

Icebows are like frozen rainbows. Sunlight is bent and reflected through ice crystals instead of raindrops. The ice crystals don't split and spread the light into a spectrum of colors, though—they're too small. So an icebow is only a white arch. Icebows are sometimes called frostbows.

Lenticular Clouds

Is a UFO landing? No, it's just a lenticular (lens-shaped) cloud. These weird-shaped clouds usually show up near mountain tops. Why? When air hits a mountain, it's forced upward toward its peak. If that air is moist, it forms clouds once it gets high enough. When waves of moist air hit a mountain, they form clouds as it climbs the mountain. The stacked-layers look of lenticular clouds comes from wave after wave of moist air making clouds as the air reaches the mountain's peak.

WEATHER SCIENTISTS IN ACTION

The sky is a big place. It takes a lot of people, equipment, and work to keep an eye on it. Weather crosses borders, so most countries around the world share the information they collect. There are about 10,000 weather stations on the seven continents. Weather stations have instruments that measure and record temperature, atmospheric pressure, humidity, wind speed, wind direction, and rainfall.

A meteorologist is a scientist who studies weather. Meteorologists continually measure, observe, record, and track what's going on in the atmosphere. Their work helps us know what weather is on the way. Measurements from weather stations provide part of the picture. Sophisticated, high-tech radar systems, weather balloons, airplanes, ocean ships, and satellites add to it. It's a big atmosphere out there.

Weather Station

(A) **A** weather vane **gives the direction of the wind.**
(B) **An** anemometer **measures wind speed.**
(C) **A** hygrometer **measures humidity.**
(D) **A** thermometer **reads air temperature and records the day's highest and lowest temperatures.**
(E) **A** barometer **measures atmospheric, or air, pressure.**
(F) **A** rain gauge **measures rainfall or snowfall amounts.**

Wind Storms

Tornadoes are storms of violently spinning air. The strongest tornadoes can have winds up to 300 mph (480 km/h), the fastest on the planet's surface. Winds this strong have the power to lift trains and smash houses. While fierce, tornadoes are short-lived local events. The average tornado lasts only a few minutes and travels only a couple of miles. Thunderstorms create tornadoes. The biggest twisters come from supercell thunderstorms. These giant, towering cumulonimbus thunderstorms soar toward the stratosphere and are many miles in diameter. Inside is a complex mixture of winds that whip up tubes of spinning air. In the spring, supercell thunderstorms are common in the Great Plains states like Texas, Oklahoma, Kansas, Nebraska, and Iowa. That's how the area earned the nickname Tornado Alley.

Tropical Storms

Tropical cyclones are called hurricanes in the Americas. But no matter where they happen, these storms are gigantic—the planet's largest. Hurricanes usually span 300 miles (480 km), making them easily seen from space as a white swirling disk with a hole in the center. Tropical cyclones are born in the warm water near the equator. The air above the warm evaporating water grows more and more humid. As the warm, moist, low-pressure air rises, it cools. Its water vapor condenses into clouds and rain. When water vapor cools to liquid droplets, it lets go of a heap of heat that goes out into the air. The warmed surrounding air then rises faster, pulling more moisture up into the storm. The hurricane becomes a growing engine fueled by heat. Once powered, the storm can move away from its tropical ocean and make landfall far from the equator. While hurricanes are known for their high winds, flooding caused by these storms is what most often destroys property and takes lives.

Texas Tragedy

In the year 1900, a hurricane flooded Galveston, Texas, killing 8,000 people.

(6.5 square km) area was destroyed. In an instant 80,000 people were homeless. The Daultipur-Salturia Tornado is the world's deadliest on record.

One 30-year-old villager told what he saw that stormy day in Bangladesh. "I saw the elephant tusk (a tornado) come down from the sky," said Mokbul Hussain. "And before I could realize, it swept away everything." Hussain's leg was broken and he suffered head injuries. But he was luckier than his wife

Corona

When the moon shining through clouds wears a crown of light, the crown is called a corona. A moon's corona is usually blue closest to the moon and turns more reddish-brown farther outward. Coronas are created by thin altocumulus clouds. Light reflecting off the moon is slightly bent by the tiny water droplets in the clouds as it passes around them, creating the disc of light.

Virga

What do you call precipitation that doesn't reach its destination? Virga. These streaks of rain or ice crystals fall out of a cloud and evaporate before reaching the ground. Virga is common in dry places like deserts where rain evaporates as it falls through dry air. These desert rain-streaks are often seen at the bottom of cumulus clouds. Fallstreaks are a kind of virga made by ice crystals falling out of high cirrus clouds. The ice crystals form wispy tail-like shapes before changing into water vapor high in the air.

Circling the Poles

Polar orbiting weather satellites circle at about 530 miles (850 km) above Earth's surface—about twice as high up as the International Space Station. Earth rotates underneath them as the satellites loop from North to South poles.

Weather balloons

Twice a day in about 800 places worldwide, meteorologists walk outdoors holding gigantic balloons and let them go. Each of these helium-filled balloons carries an instrument package called a radiosonde. It collects weather measurements as it rises up into the air and sends them back down to the weather stations on the ground. The measurements give scientists the temperature, humidity, and air pressure up into the stratosphere. The balloon eventually bursts, and the radiosonde parachutes to the ground.

Radar

Turn on the TV weather report, and everybody's talking about what's on radar. *Ra*dio *de*tecting *and* *ran*ging is what *radar* stands for. It's a technology for detecting faraway things—including weather. Radar antennae send radio waves into the air. When the waves hit raindrops, sleet, snowflakes, hail, or other precipitation in the air they bounce back to the antenna. A computer turns the echoed radio waves into a picture that shows where it's raining or snowing. Newer Doppler radar can also show wind speeds and direction. Wind conditions are important for tracking fronts and storms.

Satellites

Right now, dozens of spacecraft are watching Earth. No, it's not an alien invasion—they're weather satellites. Satellites are big-picture weather-information tools. As they orbit Earth, weather satellites send back views of clouds, storms moving across the continents, and hurricanes brewing over oceans. Satellites measure temperatures of cloud-tops, the upper atmosphere, and the oceans. They track wind speeds and invisible water vapor in the atmosphere.

High Loop

Geostationary weather satellites orbit above Earth's equator at a height of 22,400 miles (36,000 km)—about a tenth of the way to the moon. They move with our planet as it rotates eastward.

Mapping Weather

Weather information constantly collected around the world is often illustrated as maps. A kind of weather map called a synoptic chart shows current conditions in the atmosphere. Studying a sequence of weather maps shows meteorologists how the weather changes over time. It helps them make predictions about—or forecast—future weather.

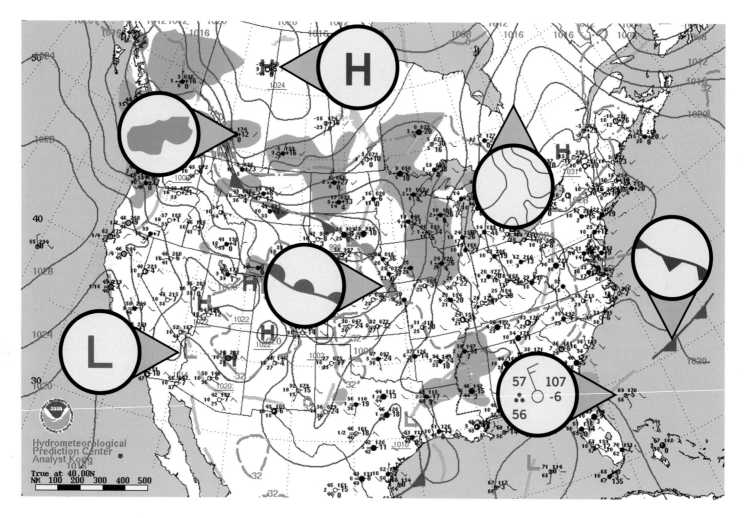

Fronts are marked with lines of blue triangles for a cold front, red semicircles for a warm front, and both mixed together for a stationary front.

H L

H stands for a high-pressure system. High atmospheric pressure often means fair weather. **L** stands for a low-pressure system, which usually means cloudy skies.

The curved line is called an isobar. It links points that have the same atmospheric pressure (the number within the isobar measures the air pressure in millibars). The closer together the isobars are, the stronger the wind.

The green shaded areas are where **precipitation** (rain, snow, etc.) is currently falling.

CRACK THE METEOROLOGICAL CODE

All those clusters of numbers and symbols on the synoptic chart are weather station plots. Each plot, no matter where it comes from, has the same standard arrangement of numbers and symbols. They show all the information gathered from a single weather station in a space-saving code. Here's what it all means:

Wind
The symbol's stem points to the direction from which the wind is blowing. In this example, the wind is coming from the north. The smaller lines attached to the stem show the speed of the wind. Wind speed is measured in knots, with each line counting for 10 knots. A knot is a speed of 11.5 mph (18.5 km/h).

Atmospheric Pressure
Numbers are tenths of millibars (mb) of pressure. Since air pressure normally ranges between 970 mb and 1040 mb, the leading 10 or 9 and the decimal point are left off to save space. So, 982 means 998.2 mb and 107 means 1,010.7.

Temperature
Given in Fahrenheit (F) or Celsius (C).

57   107

56   -6

Weather
Symbols tell what is happening right now in a particular spot, from rain or thunder to fog or mist. This symbol means it is raining.

Change in Pressure
This number shows how much the air pressure has changed in the past three hours and is reported in tenths of millibars. A -6 means the atmospheric pressure given on this plot is 0.6 mb lower than it was three hours ago. A +3 means it's 0.3 mb higher. Falling pressure often brings cloudy weather, rising pressure means clear skies.

Dew Point
When the air reaches the dew-point temperature, water vapor in the air condenses into liquid. Dew points change with both the air temperature and humidity. The closer the dew point and air temperature are to each other, the more humid it feels.

Sky Cover
The more the circle is filled in, the cloudier the sky in that area is.

On the Watch

Each dot is a forecasting office of the National Weather Service. Which one is closest to you?

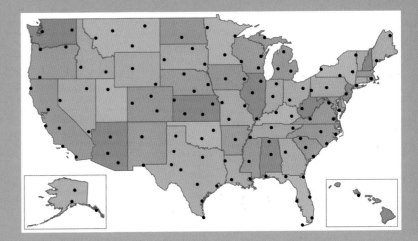

Predicting Tomorrow

Scientists are constantly collecting weather information from stations on land, boats and buoys at sea, balloons in the air, and satellites in space. But all those maps of temperatures, cloud patterns, air pressures, and wind speeds aren't created just to know what the weather is like now. Meteorologists want to know what the weather will be like later. Figuring out future weather is what forecasting is all about.

Anyone can forecast the soon-to-be weather. Look out the window. Is the Sunday morning sky sunny and clear? No rain in the next half hour is a sure-bet forecast. On the other hand, predicting what the afternoon's weather will be isn't so easy. To do so, you need to know what the sky is like over the horizon. Figuring out Monday's weather calls for a view of the atmosphere above surrounding states. And for Wednesday's forecast, seeing the air above most of the continent is necessary. This is why meteorologists need information from all over the world, all the time. All that weather information is continually fed into powerful number-crunching computers. They use complicated math equations to predict how weather conditions will likely change over the next minutes, hours, and days—creating a forecast.

Today's forecast is a surer bet than a week from today.

The Sooner the Better

The further into the future a weather forecast is, the less likely it will be right. Short-range forecasts predict the weather over the next 18 to 36 hours. They are more accurate than extended forecasts, which predict the weather over the next three or more days. What weather conditions you're predicting matters, too. Tomorrow's temperature is much easier to predict than whether it will rain or snow. The exact location of fronts can be tracked for days, but predicting when and where one will dump snow or spin out a storm is trickier.

When unexpected rain ruins a picnic, it's easy to complain about mistaken forecasts. But think about all the complex parts that go into a forecast. How is Earth's spinning changing winds? How are air masses forming over different parts of Earth as the sun heats them unequally? How much heat is being added to or taken out of the air as water changes from liquid to solid to gas? Weather forecasting is complicated!

Computers help forecasters predict weather.

Weather Power

People have put the weather to work for thousands of years. Wind powered the sailing ships of ancient Egyptians and pumped water for the Persians millennia ago. Native Americans depended on the sun to dry food, clay pots, and building bricks. Hundreds of years ago, water-powered wheels turned grain-grinding mills. In the last century, fossil fuels have taken over the job of running machines and moving people. But burning coal, natural gas, and oil have also created a lot of planet-warming pollution.

Plus our supply of fossil fuels won't last forever. Once all the petroleum is pumped out of the ground, that'll be the end of it. Today humans are looking for new and cleaner sources of energy, as well as sources that we can't run out of, called renewable energy. Some new energy technologies are going back to an old source—the weather. They're putting sun, air, and water to work making electricity. Renewable energy from the weather could solve some pollution problems and help Earth.

Shining Sun

Technology to turn sunlight into electricity was once rare. Now solar panels are everywhere, from spacecraft and houses to radios and calculators. These kinds of panels use photovoltaic (FO-toe-vahl-TAY-ik) cells. When sunlight strikes layered materials in a cell, its energy causes electric charges to flow in a current.

In super-sunny places, a different kind of solar technology can make electricity for entire cities. Solar concentrators are long, rounded troughs lined with reflectors. The reflectors tilt toward the sun and concentrate the sun's energy onto a pipe running along the center of

Panels of photovoltaic cells make electricity for this home.

the trough. A heat-absorbing liquid flows in the pipe and gets hot from the sunlight. The heated liquid in the pipe then flows to a building where it boils water into steam. The steam spins an engine, called a turbine, that generates electricity. Solar-farm power plants in the Nevada and California deserts make electricity for hundreds of thousands of homes there.

EARTH'S CHANGING CLIMATE: MODELING THE FUTURE

Human-created pollution is warming Earth's temperature. A warmer globe will melt icecaps, raise the level of the sea, and bring more extreme weather. Why do scientists think these planet-wide changes will happen? Global climate models tell them.

Global climate models (GCMs) are giant math problems that describe how Earth works. There are separate math equations for everything that affects climate—oceans, moving continents, animals, plants, ice, volcanoes, gases in the air, sunlight, and so on. Powerful supercomputers do all the calculations and combine them to create a picture of the current climate. Researchers can change one part to see how it causes the climate to change. For example, does subtracting the amount of ice in Antarctica make ocean levels rise? Does adding more greenhouses gases cause deserts to grow in size? Climate models teach us how Earth reacts to changes and show us what it might look like centuries into the future.

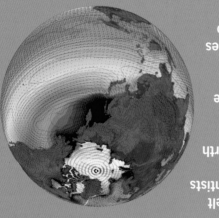

One Super Computer

Some climate-model supercomputers do more than 80 million math problems an hour.

A Powerful World of Weather

We live on a weather-filled planet. The atmosphere around us is always shifting and mixing, making new weather day in and day out. As our warming world faces climate change, some people are turning to the weather for help. Flip up this page to see how the same sun, air, and water that powers our weather, can create power for us, too.

Whirling Air

Wind power is another kind of renewable energy. A steady wind turns two or three propeller-like blades on a tall pole. The propellers spin a turbine that generates electricity. Gigantic wind-turbine farms add their electricity into a region's overall power grid, helping to power towns and businesses. There are also smaller, rooftop wind generators for homes. And you can still see old farm windmills pumping well water for livestock out in places beyond the reach of electric power lines.

Wind turbines like these are taller than the Statue of Liberty.

Falling Water

When moving water makes electricity, it's called hydroelectric power. Water flowing downward through a dam spins the blades of a turbine that generates electricity. China makes more electricity from hydroelectric dams than any other country.

People have been making electricity with waterfalls and dams for more than a century. Now inventors and engineers are looking for other ways to get power from a giant source of moving water— the ocean. Wave energy harnesses the up and down power of ocean waves. A mile or so (1.6 km) offshore a floating buoy-like turbine is anchored to the seafloor. Passing waves push and pull on machinery inside it, driving the turbine to generate electricity. Tides are also a sure source of moving water. Tidal generators are like upside windmills that turn underwater as water flows by. Like wind turbines, their blades spin a turbine that makes electricity that flows into a region's power grid.

Hoover Dam has been making electricity from the falling Colorado River since 1936.

Words to Know

air mass a very large body of air with a uniform temperature and moisture

anemometer an instrument for measuring wind speed

atmosphere the blanket of air that surrounds Earth and lies between its land or oceans and outer space

atmospheric pressure also called air pressure; the weight of the air from the ground (or water's surface) to the top of the atmosphere

aurora glowing bands of natural light seen in the night sky caused by energy particles from space hitting the atmosphere

barometer an instrument that measures atmospheric pressure, often given in millibars

cyclone an area of low atmospheric pressure surrounded by winds circling inward

Doppler radar a type of radar that uses radio frequency changes to measure wind speed and direction

extended forecast weather prediction for next three or more days

front the boundary between two different air masses

humidity the amount of water vapor in the air

hurricane a tropical cyclone on either side of the Americas with winds of at least 74 mph (119 km/h)

hygrometer an instrument that measures humidity

ionosphere the part of the atmosphere that contains many electrically charged atoms, called ions

isobars lines on a weather map connecting points of equal atmospheric pressure

meteorologist a scientist who studies weather

radar short for radio detecting and ranging, it's a technology for detecting distant objects, including rain, clouds, and storms

radiosonde a package of weather-measuring instruments that falls through the air

short-term forecast weather prediction for next 18–36 hours

tornado a violently rotating column of air coming down from a thunderstorm cloud and in contact with the ground

tropical cyclone powerful, rotating ocean storm with high winds

Find Out More

Websites to Visit

FEMA for Kids
www.fema.gov/kids/tornado.htm
The Federal Emergency Management Agency's site for kids about storm safety. Get in the know and get ready!

Climate-Change Kids' Sites
www.epa.gov/climatechange/kids/
http://climate.nasa.gov/kids/
Find out more about climate change—and what to do about it—at these sites.

Franklin's Forecast
http://www.fi.edu/weather/
The Franklin Institute's weather website has everything from how to make your own weather instruments to reading Doppler radar.

Dan's Wild Weather Page
http://www.wildwildweather.com
Meteorologist Dan Satterfield takes you through a bunch of weather topics.

Web Weather
http://eo.ucar.edu/webweather/
Play weather games such as Lightning Trivia, learn the cloud types, and more.

Bibliography

Williams, Jack. *The Weather Book: An Easy-to-Understand Guide to the US's Weather.* New York: Vintage, 1997.

National Weather Service. JetStream—Online Weather School. http://www.srh.noaa.gov/jetstream/

U.S. Department of Energy. Renewable Energy. http://www.energysavers.gov/renewable_energy

Online Meteorology Guide. WW2010™, University of Illinois website. http://ww2010.atmos.uiuc.edu

Source Notes

Page 20: "The jet streams mark. . . . tropics are getting wider.": "Faster Atmospheric Warming in Subtropics Pushes Jet Streams Toward Poles." *University of Washington News*, May 25, 2006. http://uwnews.org/article.asp?articleid=24603

Page 37: "I saw the . . . I do not know.": "Storms Bring Death, Damage as Drought End in Bangladesh." *Seattle Times.* April 27, 1989.

Index

48